Sleep Paralysis

Michael Beloved

Proofreader: Marcia Beloved

Shiva Art: Sir Paul Castagna

Illustrations: Sir Paul Castagna/author

Castagna's art is signed with ©

Correspondence:

Michael Beloved   Paul Castagna
18311 NW 8th Street   204 Northern Sophie
Pembroke Pines   Bessemer
FL 33029   MI 49911
USA   USA

Email: axisnexus@gmail.com

ISBN: **978-0-9840013-6-1**

LCCN: **2012913595**

Table of Contents

Introduction *6*

Chapter 1 .... *7*

   Sleep Paralysis Described 7

Chapter 2 .... *25*

   Psychological Components 25

Chapter 3 .... *40*

   Reduction of Incidences 40

Chapter 4 .... *57*

   Sorting an Event 57

Chapter 5 .... *68*

   Realization of the Subtle Body 68

Chapter 6 .... *73*

   Sleep Paralysis Reversed 73

Artist's Closing Remarks *80*

Glossary *83*

Index *85*

Author *97*

Publications *99*

   English Series 99

   Meditation Series 103

Explained Series 104

Commentaries...106

Specialty 111

Online Resources...114

How to use this book:

Make a casual reading page for page without becoming stressed about the concepts and ideas. Read to become familiar with the language style and presentation. If you read something of particular interest make a mental note and read on to get through the entire book.

Make a second reading pausing at areas of interest, where you feel you can grasp the material. Here and there, you may not follow the meanings but read on nevertheless.

Make a third reading with intent to grasp the concepts and suggestions given.

Finally, make an indepth study of this information.

Introduction

Sleep Paralysis is a big topic in cyberspace. It rates with astral projection and lucid dreaming. It is an old human ailment of the psychic sorts. It is linked to epilepsy, a nerve malfunction which remains a mystery even to medical professionals.

This booklet details experiences and solutions which the author used to decrease sleep paralysis incidences. For him this began in childhood. At the time it seemed to be a natural part of human psychology.

Even as a child he studied it secretly. Later when he practiced meditation, he reached the conclusions which are shared in this booklet.

Chapter 1

Sleep Paralysis Described

This condition occurs when the subtle body, the dream casing, does not synchronize into the physical body in a completely harmonious way. This may occur on the verge of sleeping and on the verge of waking or during the state between sleep and waking condition or even between waking and sleeping conditions. The puzzle about sleep paralysis is that its cause is a malfunction in consciousness which nature operates.

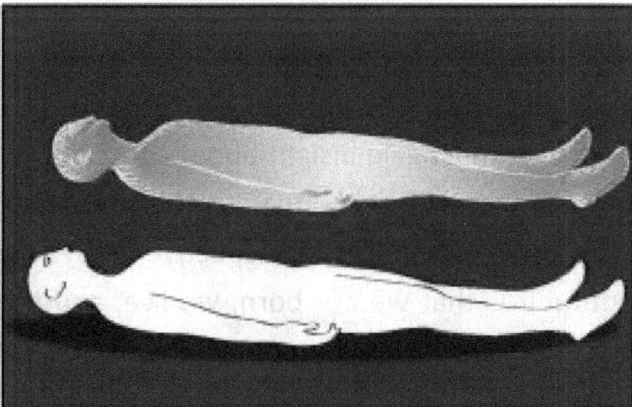

We take birth by functions of nature. We sleep and wake mostly by the operative functions of nature. These instances are not what we normally operate. Thus when we are about to wake up and we cannot, we become puzzled because the normal system of rising which nature operated previously for our convenience, malfunctioned.

Some of us are affected by sleep paralysis from childhood. We go through life struggling to control it. Some others experience it once in a while. And yet there are some who have never experienced it and wonder if the tales about it are imaginative dreams.

Sleep paralysis is a real condition. It eludes us because we are born through functions of nature which are beyond our control but which we are dependent upon. How can we come to grips with this? Is it possible to take command of some of these nature-controlled psychological operations?

First we must gain insight about consciousness before we can effectively manage the controllable parts of it. This requires introspective study. How beautiful it is that we are born, we live, and then supposedly we die, all by nature operations. The magic of it!

Humans went into outer space. Some visited the moon. Yet, we have no clear schematic of consciousness. Most accomplishments in the realm of consciousness were achieved by ingesting chemicals of nature, which allowed us to put living bodies to sleep for surgery and to experience altered states by effects of chemicals on the brain cells.

Can we do anything else to clarify the geography of consciousness?

It is an individual pursuit. We can sit and discuss our experiences but it is not like when you meet physically, plan an experiment, do it, observe the results of it and file a scientific report. Psychic research by its very nature occurs on the individual level within the psyche of the person concerned.

To begin this conversation, I present the premise that there is a subtle body which is used in realistic dreams that are more than just imagination in the mind. There are visions and sounds in the mind, which are triggered by imagination but there are also factual occurrences which take place in subtle dimensions.

This vision in the mind of a sleeping child
is triggered by desire, memory and imagination.
Even though based on reality,
it is only as real
as the mental substance in the mind

This child's subtle body separated
from the physical form.
It is in a realistic astral dimension
which is not the child's mental creation

These subtle locations are called the astral world. Some call it the realm of the hereafter. Some say it is the place for the afterlife. What I am concerned with is my status in that alternate reality. Consider it as the background world, the place which is the foundation for physical existence. We begin this discourse by admitting a subtle body which is used in realistic dreams. This body may be called the dream body, the subtle body, the astral projection body and even the shadow body, the etheric body, the energy body, the mind body, the mento-emotional body, the psychological content body or the psychic body.

The physical body is defined by the substances which comprise it. These materials are kept in order in a skin, which is a near-airtight bag. What are the components of the subtle body? It comprises subtle energy, astral stuffs and the stuffs of an individual's psychology. It is made of the stuff of reason, the stuff of thinking, the stuff of feeling and the stuff of sensation.

It may be called the body which is the form of the individual's psychology. Imagine your emotions, mental force and sensations, all formed into a body. What would that be? How will that be shaped? What will be its color? That is the subtle body. That is the astral form. That is the system in you which has dream experiences.

This subtle body is neatly and efficiently packed into the physical body so that if the two forms separate, their reunion should naturally take place without a hitch, without even your observation of how that takes place. However sleep paralysis may be viewed as an occasion when you are forced to distinguish the two bodies.

In sleep paralysis when someone is about to awaken, that person discovers that there is a difference between the subtle body and the physical one. However the discovery may be veiled with misunderstanding. This is because some of us assume that there is no subtle body. We feel that we are the physical body. When we are obstructed from using it, we feel that our person is inconvenienced.

Usually when I rise from sleep, everything happens in a particular order, the same order which I always experienced since I became aware of myself as the material body. In that system, I feel that I am the physical body. However, consider that this natural process is one of misidentification. This happened because the identity energy carries no impression of itself. Instead it carries the properties of whatever it is fused into or superimposed upon.

When the subtle body is separated out of the physical one, we experience a dream world which is a subtle existence all unto itself. This is different from when we experience a dream in the mind. In other words, there can be a dream in the mind in the brain, and in contrast to that, there can be a

dream   outside   of   the   mind   in   a   subtle
environment.

This sleeper is dreaming in the mind.
Using the psychic substance of desire and memory
the imagination of this dreamer creates
scenes which yield pleasure

This sleeper's astral body has separated
out of the physical form.
As his astral self he met a woman
whose astral body also separated
from her physical form
They conduct romantic affairs in a subtle dimension.

   There are imaginary dreams in the mind space,
in the brain space. These fantasies are creations of
the mind. These are the same as when one
visualizes scenes in the mind. But these are not the

same as actual astral performance which takes place in a real astral landscape.

Just as I can imagine a fruit in my mind, and there may be no real fruit before me, so one can imagine a dream in the mind and not be in a real astral place. But all the same I can have an actual fruit and eat that, and I can be in a real astral place and experience subtle reality in it.

One should get rid of the idea that every dream experience is an imaginary. Only some are. The problem is to be able to distinguish those astral experiences which take place in a real astral dimension and those imaginations which take place only because something is visualized in the mind.

To distinguish visualization in the mind from a real astral experience, we must use the same discernment which is used when we segregate an imagined idea of a physical substance from an actual object which exists independent of imagination, as in the case of imagining an apple and actually having one in my hand which can be shared with another person.

This also requires self-honesty. Can you trust yourself so that you can discern when you are imagining something and when something is independent of your imagination and is therefore a real substance which is not reliant on your perception? We can easily do this with physical objects. With subtle objects we can train ourselves to do this.

For physical honesty we use the perceptions of others, so that if I say I have an apple, and others cannot confirm that I do, then I can realize my delusion. With subtle perception, it depends mostly on my self-honesty. Others cannot easily penetrate my imaginative or real astral experiences. That is mostly reliant on self-honesty.

When you as a subtle body cannot take control of the physical body, that is called sleep paralysis. Since you assumed yourself as the physical body, this lack of control is uncomfortable if not downright spooky. You need to begin seeing yourself as the subtle body which tries to reawaken or make alive the sleeping physical form. If that form does not respond to you as it normally did, that is the condition of sleep paralysis. This can happen when you are going to sleep or when you are rising after having slept.

The preferred situation is that when you are about to sleep, you lose awareness of yourself as a physical body and you may then find yourself in dreams, either real ones or mental creations which your sleepy mind composed. The other preferred situation is that when you are to rise, you find yourself awake as your physical body, and you then experience the concluding scenes of a dream or you just find yourself awake as a physical body with no recollection of dreams. Sleep paralysis is when this occurs with an inconvenienced feeling that you cannot operate the physical body. This is not because your physical body had a stroke or nerve failure. It is because your astral or subtle form desynchronized from the physical one. Your willpower could no longer operate the physical limbs because it was not connected through the brain and nervous system of the physical system.

If during sleep paralysis, there is a loud noise or if for instance someone touches your body or jerks it, then the sleep paralysis ends abruptly. You wake up as the physical you in control of the motor functions of that body. What actually happened, however, is that the physical body was jolted into synchronization with the subtle form. The disturbance of the loud voice, touch or jerk, caused the natural psycho-physical fusion to occur instantly putting both bodies into sync.

What is the mechanism which does this?

For one thing it cannot be a mere physical reality. It cannot be merely a subtle or psychological operation either. It has to be physical and psychological simultaneously. Why is that system functioning correctly some of the time? Why does it malfunction on occasion thus causing the inconvenience of not being able to operate the motor functions?

Sleep paralysis is the inability of the person to operate the physical body. This occurs because the psychological part of the person is not in sync with the physical body of the person.

Normally the person can command the motor functions upon awakening after sleep. When sleep paralysis occurs, the person's willpower remains operative except that it fails to inspire the motor functions. This results in a distressful condition and a feeling of disempowerment.

There is a subtle body which is distinct from the physical form. This is also known as an astral body. When this body is separated from the physical one, a person may or may not be conscious of the separation. Most people do not become conscious of the separation. It is natural not to be conscious of it. Some persons, who are psychically sensitive, describe their experience of the separation.

In any case the separation becomes evident during sleep paralysis. Then it is an unpleasant experience because of the lack of control of the motor functions. A spooky otherworld experience might also occur during sleep paralysis. The dreamer might mistake that as part of the paralysis even though it occurred coincidentally.

I will now objectively define sleep paralysis. Take the definition at face value even if you think that you are your material body and nothing else. If you feel that your psychological self is part of yourself as the physical body, keep that understanding but have an open mind to what I explain:

Sleep paralysis is the condition of not being able to operate the physical body even though one is conscious within that body. This condition usually occurs when one is just about to wake up as the physical body or when one is just about to sleep in nature's process of suspended wakefulness.

There are two bodies. One is physical. The other is the subtle form which comprises the *psychology of the person*. This subtle body is used in imaginative and realistic dreams. When the two bodies are fused together, the subtle one is interspaced into the physical one. When they are not, the subtle body is separated out of the physical one. This separation may be experienced rarely or frequently according to a person's developed or undeveloped psychic perception.

Persons, who experience the subtle body objectively when it is separated from the physical one, describe that as astral projection, which means that the subtle form was projected out of or away from the physical system. When someone experiences the subtle existence while the subtle body is interspaced in the physical one, that is called a lucid dreaming or psychic experience.

During a lucid experience if the person desires to operate the physical body and cannot do so, then that is a sleep paralysis. It is very important that you accept my premise which is that there are two bodies. Each of these is distinctly separate from the other, just as electricity is separate from the copper wire in which it is transmitted.

The subtle body is similar to electricity. The current which travels through a copper wire, causes the armature of a motor to spin but if the motor does not spin, we consider that to be a malfunction. In the same way if when awakening, the physical body does not respond to my commands for movement, it is called a sleep paralysis malfunction.

If a motor does not spin, we may call an electrician. He may locate the defective circuit and correct it. However it is not that simple when fixing a malfunction between the subtle body and the physical one. Trying to fix the sleep paralysis all by yourself is similar to the electricity in the copper wire trying to determine how to repair a component in the motor circuits.

Even though electricity is the primary cause of motion in the motor, it cannot repair a malfunction. It may detect when the motor does not spin because its current does not flow as it did when the motor was in order. We know there is something wrong when there is a sleep paralysis but like the electricity we cannot then determine the problem. Most of all even if we can analyze the malfunction we may not be in an existential position to rectify it.

Chapter 2

Psychological Components

To solve the problem of sleep paralysis, some medical researcher may discover a drug which could be applied to the body of a person who is restrained. That solution would depend on someone knowing that a spirit's subtle form was unable to move its physical system. Therein lies the difficulty of a medical approach. Medical professionals are baffled enough by the condition of patients who are in a coma and who from all indications can hear but cannot respond sufficiently to describe their inner condition.

I will describe other approaches which worked for me, methods which I figured out on my own. These may or may not work for you but the information will enable you to better understand what happens during an event.

I began having sleep paralysis sessions during childhood. I never mentioned it to my relatives but struggled with it alone. I assumed it was something that each person had to deal with without getting assistance from others. There were other events which I considered in that way. For instance learning to walk and then miscalculating distances and falling, learning to run, then running so fast that one foot obstructed the other, then stumbling, falling with a crash and bruising my knees.

Dreaming, the astral world, suspicion of the dark, hesitancy to enter dark graveyards, were all part of my childhood which I did not feel the necessity to share with others. I assumed every human being and even some animals had to deal with these experiences on their own.

As a child, I figured to myself that spirits existed in the atmosphere and were not to be interfered with unless one had a special issue with them. I used to see beings in the astral world during dream sessions. I thought that the dream side of life was real and that it was natural to be participating in its history during sleeping hours, just as I got involved on the physical side during waking times.

When my body was about 9 years of age, I had an experience which caused me to review these experiences. I was taking a nap and it was high noon. I lived in a location which was about 6 degrees north of the equator. The sun was overhead.

During the nap I found myself getting larger and larger beyond the size of my material body. I was getting larger and larger and could not control the increasing sizes. I got so large that I was larger than the planet. I was out in space and even though I could feel myself as this larger-than-the-earth body, I could not see it. I felt it to be substantial, not flimsy, but it was either transparent or my vision was not in the dimension of its mass. I looked down on the earth and began wishing that I was the nine year old boy and not the gigantic body.

Just then I began getting smaller and smaller, until I was looking at my body lying on a bed. Then suddenly it all ended and I was again that small body. I was relieved. I thought to myself, "God must be like that. This is weird!"

As soon as I thought this, I remembered having the experience before but I could not pinpoint the memory. It was a different type of memory. It was not normal memory which I used from day to day in the nine-year old body.

I never shared the experience with anyone. I used to have experiences where I would be trying to wake up, especially during a day nap. I would be trying to wake up as me, as the kid, but I could not wake up. I would be in my body and would be struggling to move it. It simply would not budge. Then suddenly I would wake up. On some occasions, I would wake up for about 3 seconds and then slip back into the powerless state of sleep paralysis again.

This happened regularly but after the enlarging experience, I remembered that it happened before even though prior to that I did not make a special note of these experiences.

Time went by. This experience used to occur frequently. I developed a method of getting out of sleep paralysis. It was a breath suspension action. It seems that even though I could not operate any of the limbs of the body, nor the vocal cord, I could hold the breath for a time. If I held it long enough, I snapped out of the sleep paralysis and woke up. This worked about 9 out of 10 times. I noticed however that even if I failed to snap out of it, it went away by itself, usually after about 40 seconds for the most.

I used to hear stories about spirit possession of infants, where it was said that old higues, vampire spirits, would suck the bodies of infants.

To prevent this, people took asafetida and pasted it in the hair of the would-be victim. The smell of the condiment kept the old higue away, or at least that is what people believed. The idea was that when a woman gets very old, say beyond the age of 80, her body no longer produced blood. To live she had to acquire blood from infants.

I was never fearful of old higues but I knew that spirits were for real because I used to see them, especially at night during the time when my relatives hardly used electricity. When my body was about 16 years of age, I realized that I knew more about the spirit world than most adults. I wondered about this.

Later when my body was about 20 years of age, I was in the Philippines and I decided to write a book explaining sleep paralysis and astral projection. By that time, I knew that my psychic perception was uncommon. When people asked me about astral projection, I would describe to them how it happens, meaning how nature causes it to happen, and how a human being can facilitate nature to make it happen more frequently. I was never of the view that astral projection was mainly caused by the individual. My experience was that nature operates it all by itself with or without the assistance of the individual.

I began to read about the astral experiences of others. I studied books on the subject. I learned yoga postures and meditation techniques. I spoke to some mystics. One such book which impressed me initially was the *Third Eye* by T. Lobsang Rampa.

I decided to study astral projection and sleep paralysis in more detail. First of all I knew that sleep paralysis was part of astral projection and was not a separate occurrence. For me sleep paralysis only occurred when my astral body was either leaving the physical system or getting back into it. A failed reentry was the state of physical non-response to commands of my will power.

From this I understood one thing clearly. If the subtle body and the physical one were out of sync and I was conscious of this, it caused a panic and a scary feeling due to not being able to operate the physical system.

This meant to me that the system which controlled the distinction and union of the two bodies malfunctioned and was not under the control of the individual concerned. In childhood I had no idea how I could fix this. It never crossed my mind to discuss this with adults.

Once after a session of sleep paralysis which happened after my subtle body tried to fuse into the physical system, a senior relative asked me if I had a bad dream. Apparently she noticed that my breath was irregular while sleeping. I replied, "Yes," and dropped the matter there. I once asked a school friend about his experiences but he looked at me as if it was something strange. He did ask, however, if I was being haunted by a jumbie, which is a creole word for a mischievous disembodied spirit.

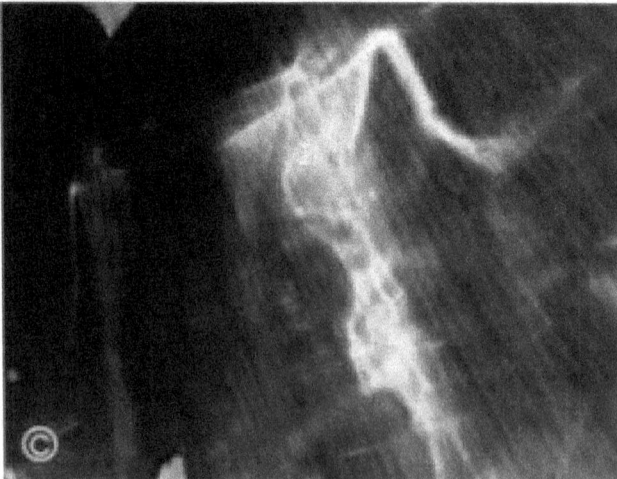

At this time, under the age of 13, I surmised all by myself that there were at least four factors involved in existence:

1. material body
2. subtle body
3. psychic mechanism which controlled the fission and fusion of the material and subtle forms
4. spirit individual

At the time I did not think of reincarnation, I was content with the idea that you were either dead or alive but being dead only meant being transferred permanently into the spirit world, the astral existence. To me you were either a subtle body using a corresponding physical system or you were a subtle body without such a system and then you lived only in the astral world, which physical people only visit at night when the physical system sleeps.

The four components which I mentioned above were to me the factors involved in a sleep paralysis experience. But there was one other thing: the breath mechanism. It was a part of the physical body to be sure but it was special. You could hold the breath. That forced the two bodies into fusion, ending the sleep paralysis.

I used to hold my breath for as long as I could and then I would snap out of the paralysis. In other words, when I found myself as the subtle body unable to move the physical one, I had control over one thing in the physical system. That was the breath. If I held it long enough, the physical body jerked slightly and the two bodies fused, so that I got up, as usual, as a physical person.

It was with this knowledge that I stumbled upon information about the kundalini life force. This was information from yoga teachers and from books from India which described mysticism according to the yoga tradition. I had already experienced the kundalini, sometimes as a shivering of my body, with electric sensations moving up my spine, or sudden dizziness in the head. When I read about it in the yoga books, I began to realize my experiences even more and was able to make sense of these subtle events.

According to yogic lore the life force or kundalini is stationed at the base of the spine. This force operates the body. It controls the sleep-wake cycle. It is responsible for the fission and fusion of the subtle and gross bodies. It is said that when the subtle body is away from the physical one, that subtle body remains connected to the physical one by a silver cord, an energy transmission line. If an alarm sounds when the two bodies are separated, the kundalini uses that transmission line to yank the subtle body back into fusion with the physical system. Thus the person wakes up suddenly as his or her physical body.

I began to study about the kundalini, reading books about it. I remember being impressed by a book which was written by Gopi Krishna but in that book I was not getting to the bottom of the subject, so I kept reading on and on. I saw posters with chakras, which are energy vortexes which were described in yoga books from India.

Luckily for me once when I was in Kansas City, Missouri, I saw a poster with a notice about lessons in kundalini yoga. The teacher was supposed to be a bearded Indian man named Yogi Bhajan. I went to the lessons but to my disappointment the yogi was not there. His disciple was there. I took lesson for about 4 afternoon sessions and then I left for Denver Colorado, where some months later I entered their teaching school as a boarding resident. This place was called an ashram.

It was here that I learned the formal system of kundalini yoga which consisted of a rapid breathing process called bhastrika pranayama. This causes the kundalini to rise up through the spine and enter the head. It is very similar to a sexual orgasm experience, except that the sensations are primarily in the spine and brain, rather than in the lower spine and genitals.

By doing the breathing process, I learned more about the kundalini's dependence on breath. I realized that this was the reason I came out of sleep paralysis by holding the breath. It seems that the kundalini panics if it cannot get access to breath. Thus if during a sleep paralysis session, one can hold the breath, the kundalini will be compelled to move forcibly to gain control of the lungs and that is enough to cause the fusion of the two bodies.

In this chapter, I explained how I reached the point of understanding my own sleep paralysis, how I tracked it through discovery that holding the breath can end it, and how I gained experience about the operation of the kundalini in the body.

Previously I listed four components of the psyche. These are:

1. material body
2. subtle body
3. psychic mechanism which controlls the fission and fusion of the material and subtle forms
4. spirit individual

The third listed item is the kundalini life force. Breath retention, which I mentioned as my main way of getting out of a sleep paralysis, is conducted by the life force but when the subtle body is partially fused into the physical one, that subtle form can gain control of the breath. In other words the person's will power can commandeer the breath which is normally controlled by the kundalini's automatic regulator system. This means that the link between the subtle body and the physical body is the kundalini and since the breath is its physical lifeline, control of the breath can affect how the kundalini operates.

Assuming that the kundalini life-force system is the cause of sleep paralysis, it is only left to figure a way to adjust this kundalini so as to eliminate most of the sleep paralysis occurrences.

We cannot expect to conquer nature 100%, but if we can get more control, then that is an achievement.

How can we target this kundalini life force? As I said previously one can get out of a sleep paralysis if one holds the breath. One should hold it until it seems that the system will panic or it will jerk. If this happens then the paralysis will cease and one will rise as normal as one's material body.

A question arises as to where the kundalini life force is located. However this question is not helpful. In fact to be successful with this procedure, one does not need to know where the life force is located. One should know that it controls the breathing system and the involuntary actions which take place in the body, like digestion and blood distribution.

To understand kundalini in the application of sleep paralysis, you only need to know that if you override and take control of the breathing system and stop the system from breathing, then the kundalini life force will act in a forceful way to fuse the subtle and physical bodies so that you can rise normally.

You only need to know that the breathing system is normally controlled by the life force. If you take control of it by stopping it so that there is no inhaling or exhaling, then the kundalini will act. That response will cause it to fuse the bodies so that you can rise as you normally do.

If you have some difficulty with the concept of a life force, then you may apply this advice anyway, with the consideration that the involuntary breathing system of the body can be used to cause your release from sleep paralysis.

Chapter 3

Reduction of Incidences

I found several methods which cause a reduction of the incidences of sleep paralysis. I do not think that any of these can completely remove all incidences. They can however singly or conjointly reduce the occurrences.

During childhood I had the view that the incidences could be reduced by just not getting into them in the first place but this is a child's simple solution which cannot deal with a complex issue. After some time, when I was a teenager, I began to abandon that view, sensing that it is not possible to totally eliminate sleep paralysis. This is because one can hardly predict with accuracy when it would happen. Even if one could predict that, one has to sleep on a daily basis. One does not have the power to stop sleeping forever. Therefore the idea of never ever entering paralysis states is impractical.

To date, I have not found a method which completely stopped sleep paralysis from occurring. I want to emphasize that. I discovered methods which reduce the frequency of the incidences. Here is a list of those procedures.

✓ Stop viewing horror movies
✓ Stop drinking alcohol
✓ Secure fresh air access for the sleeping body
✓ Stop eating late at night
✓ Avoid low-vibration association
✓ Stop use of opiates, cocaine, marijuana and psychoactive substances

Stop viewing horror movies

Once as a teenager, when I used to go to movies, I noticed that sleep paralysis occurrences noticeably increased after seeing a horror show. I gradually came to dislike spooky shows for that reason. It took about 4 years after I observed this to completely stop viewing such shows. For some reason I was attracted to those shows even though I realized that they resulted in terrible dreams and in ghastly sleep paralysis experiences with demons.

This sleeper is dreaming in the mind.
Using the psychic substance
of memory and unresolved emotions
the imagination of this dreamer creates
scenes which yeild horror.

Stop drinking alcohol

The second method which I developed had to do with drinking alcohol. I grew up in an environment where you were expected to drink alcohol to prove your maturity and independence from parents. My father was an alcoholic. Alcohol ruined much of his life and caused him to be irresponsible towards his first wife and children. I took note of that even when I was a juvenile.

Later I linked the use of alcohol to the increase in incidences of sleep paralysis. For that matter sometimes when my father would be drunk out of his wits, he would be in sleep paralysis and would be struggling to get out of it. I did not realize at the time but in retrospect I realize this.

For me, I identified the effect of alcohol when I had my first bit of vodka. I once travelled with a Russian friend from one city to another in the United States. He wanted to buy me a drink as there was a Russian tradition that friends should drink together. I had drunk beer and whiskey before but I had never drunk vodka. I was surprised when it first entered my mouth but I did not show any distaste for it because I wanted to express appreciation to my Russian friend. By the time I could get down one mixed drink, he downed three and procured even more. The guy was a pro.

At first my head started to spin and the taste of it was just not what I expected. I felt that it was something no human being should taste. Later when I slept I had several bouts with sleep paralysis. I would be in a dream and be in sleep paralysis, I would take myself out of it by holding my breath, and then I would immediately be captured in sleep paralysis and find myself in the same dream again.

After this happened I reviewed my use of alcohol over the years. I found that anytime I consumed more than one beer, it affected my subtle body in such a way as to interfere with its separation from and fusion into the physical body. I decided then and there to stop using liquor.

Secure fresh air access for the sleeping body

The third method is to make sure that there is adequate ventilation, adequate fresh air, when the physical body sleeps. I discovered this when I was in Denver, Colorado during the winter season when it is very cold, like in January. In such circumstances people usually close windows to keep heat within the living spaces. There is supposed to be central heat which means a ventilation system which provides heated fresh air. It so happens that this system of central heat varies from house to house. In some houses the filtration and generation of this air might be breached.

I discovered that if my body did not get fresh air, sleep paralysis occurred more frequently. Later this began to make more sense when I practiced kundalini yoga breath infusion methods, where I perceived how the life force in the body used fresh air. The physical body can survive on very little fresh air but when it does so, the subtle body becomes de-energized. One has more trashy dreams, and finds oneself in lower astral dimensions more frequently. Some persons have absolutely no dream recall because their bodies absorb the least amount of fresh air.

As I became more and more proficient in breath infusion techniques, I developed sensitivity such that I could not stay in a place where the air was stagnant and where the air was stale air which was already breathed by human beings or animals. I noticed that many others were not in the least bit disturbed by this. While I sensed when the proportion of fresh air in a building is decreased, others happily breathed the increased percentage of stale air without even knowing that they did so.

Once when I was meditating with a group of practitioners, we were in a building in which there was no ventilation. There was an old carpet in the building which gave off a poisonous gas which had accumulated in the building. When we got into the building, the leader of the meditation group closed the main door for privacy and to keep out extraneous noises. Immediately I felt that there was no fresh air. I remained with them through the meditation session but it took 2 days to breathe out the chemicals which were taken into my system. No one else in the session was bothered by this which meant that their bodies could tolerate the reduction of fresh air.

Persons whose systems limit the distribution of fresh air are instinctively drawn into living situations where they can be deprived of fresh air. In addition their lungs function in such a way as to absorb very small amounts of fresh air. Their lung cells discriminate and restrict the amount of fresh air getting to the cells in the body. The result of this is either more sleep paralysis occurrences or none at all but with a total shutdown of their memory of dreams. These persons are the ones who do not recall dreams and who therefore conclude that they do not have dreams.

I always made sure that there was fresh air reaching my sleeping body. I did this by always having some way to get fresh air into the room where I lay down to rest. If however one's lung system is genetically biased to restrict fresh air, one may have no idea of it. Then more than likely one will be a person who admits to no dreams, which really means that one has no recall of dreams.

The essence of this is: If the life force does not get a certain percentage of fresh air, it cannot operate the psychic memory system which operates dream observation, notation and recall. Thus for that person there will be no conscious participation in astral encounters. Such persons are having astral experiences but like one who sleepwalks, there is no memory of the activities and thus no admission of the participation.

Stop eating late at night

I tracked eating late at night as an indirect cause of increased incidences of sleep paralysis. Fortunately for me, I grew up in a social situation where the main meal for the day was at noon. In the evening around 6 or 7 pm, the last meal was tea or milk with bread, cheese and butter. That was it. There was no heavy meal in the evening. Later after I lived in a developed country, I noticed that the main meal for the day was in the evening. For some time, I followed this method. I found however that it was uncomfortable. My stomach seemed distended and hard at night. It ached during the night. I would frequently wake up during the night with attention on my intestines as there was a creeping pain there as food moved through the system. This disturbed my rest. It also affected me in a way where I went into frequent sleep paralysis because of the fatigue and weariness of mind.

After noticing this I ceased eating heavy meals at night and resumed my childhood habit of eating the main meal during the daytime. The life force processes food. If it has to process food during the night when the astral body is separated from it, it will take an action which decreases dream recall, and which may cause sleep paralysis. The more the life force is engaged in physical activities during resting, the more likely chance there is for sleep paralysis or alternately no sleep paralysis, no dream recall and a full blackout during sleep.

This blackout is a form of massive ignorance but it is beneficial to the system because then the life force may abandon high energy mental activities and concentrate on food processing and cell repair in the physical body.

Avoid low-vibration association

For me, associating with low energy persons was another cause of increased incidences. By low energy persons, I mean persons who are habitually depressed, persons who are chronic alcoholics, persons who are addicted to prescription and non-prescription drugs, especially cocaine and opium derived substances, persons whose life circumstances cause them to be living in very unclean conditions, persons who have bouts of epilepsy, mental delirium and manic states of depression.

For some reason after being with such persons and being open to their energy or being affectionate to them, I used to find myself in astral situations with them. These experiences would conclude with a sleep paralysis. My conclusion about this is that my astral body was lowered in vibration in their association, and that caused it to adopt a vibration which was incompatible with the fusion process of the two forms.

By doing meditation, I learned how to repel association with such persons and not be lowered to their astral vibratory rate.

Are these the only methods of decreasing the incidences of sleep paralysis? I personally feel that there are other ways of doing this but these are the methods which I discovered, researched and tested over the years. I encourage you to find the causes of it in your own experience. My information may provide impetus for your increased observation of the causes in your own experience.

Stop the use of opiates, cocaine, marijuana, psychoactive substances and mind-altering prescription drugs

I traced increased incidences to the use of marijuana and to some extent the use of hallucinogenic drugs. The worst, however, is the use of prescription or non-prescription opiates. These are derivatives of opium or synthetic chemicals which mimic the psychological adjustments induced by opiates.

Psychoactive drugs reset the operations of the life force, such that its usual activities may be postponed, accelerated or shut down completely. Under such influence, the life force loses its traditional discrimination and is unable to operate the body in the normal way. Many people who use prescription drugs are confident that they are doing nothing illegal. This confidence destroys their ability to properly analyze the effects of the drugs.

It does not matter if a drug is legally or illegally acquired, it will affect the life force for better or worse. In fact one may not be able to assess the effects of a certain drug. For instance, many people take drugs which cause constipation but they are unable to trace the condition to the drug because the influence of the substance is subtle. Constipation is an indirect cause of sleep paralysis. It may also cause a lack of dream recall.

Drugs affect the performance of the life force. Opiates and other chemical painkillers and nerve-impulse shutdown drugs increase dull astral consciousness, the result of which is no dream recall or low-level astral reach with increased incidence of sleep paralysis.

Chapter 4

Sorting an Event

Many persons equate sleep paralysis with demon possession. In ancient times and to some extent today, persons who have epileptic bouts are considered to be possessed by a demon during the seizures. Undoubtedly there is such a thing as demon possession but much of what is labeled in that way has nothing to do with demons.

In discussing sleep paralysis over the years, I have formed the conclusion that most people cannot sort a sleep paralysis session from the spooky events which occur during the paralysis phase. They confuse the events which occur during a sleep paralysis with the paralysis itself.

If you are such a person, your first step in dealing with these occurrences is to sort which part is the paralysis and which part is the spooky event. You can be sure that sleep paralysis is spooky in itself but it is not a ghastly event which occurs simultaneously.

Suppose I ingested a psychoactive drug which caused the life force's operations to be altered. I then fall asleep. While sleeping I have a dream which is a real astral event in which a demon chases me with intent to harm. I then try to wake up as my physical body to escape from the astral realm. I find that my physical body does not respond to my will power. The demon is coming with intentions to assault me. I freak out, scream loudly and wake up as my physical body in a scared state of mind.

Is the incidence of the demon chasing me, identical to the one of the sleep paralysis condition? Did the demon cause the sleep paralysis?

You may agree that these are not identical but they are coincidental. Usually I would wake up even without having to scream loudly. Luckily in that situation the effort to scream jerked the physical system enough to cause it to fuse back with the astral form.

For a few seconds, the paralysis condition prevented me from escaping from the astral world by the usual method of re-identifying with my physical body. The demon who chased me did not cause the paralysis condition. And yet, I may conclude that the demon arranged all of that but this would be a hasty and faulty analysis of the situation.

In a non-spooky incidence, there would be no demon chasing me, nothing would be happening out of the astral ordinary. In cases like this I can understand what the sleep paralysis is all by itself.

How do I handle a non-spooky incidence? First of all as soon as one is aware that one exists but one lacks the power to animate the physical body, one should realize then and there that one's personality is different to the physical system. One's personality is a psychological unit not a physical body. One's personality is not operating the physical body because if it did it would have to remain as the physical body always and would never be able to experience even one astral projection or objective dream experience.

If the sleep paralysis experience can be seen for what it is, which is that a personality is unable to control its physical habitat, then we can make progress and actually benefit existentially from the experience. Many of us are not certain if we will continue after death of the physical body. We are uncertain as to whether our ancestors have gone to an afterlife. This unknown condition can be removed by proper analysis of the components of a sleep paralysis session. These components are:

❖ A physical body which cannot be operated.

❖ A person who is aware of the physical body and of his or her inability to move that form.

❖ A hidden malfunctioning fusion system which usually unifies the person with the physical body when sleep is ended.

One can benefit greatly from the sleep paralysis experience if one stops to analyze the components of the experience. It is obvious what the physical body is. It is obvious when you are aware within it and cannot operate it. Thus the physical body is the most self-evident part of the experience.

Usually in these experiences, the person is so engaged in trying to move the physical body, in trying to be the physical system as usual, that there is no consideration that the person is something apart from and independent of the physical body. Train yourself to stop during a sleep paralysis and consider that you, the person, are not the body even though you, the person, are being deprived of the right to be the body, to wake up as the physical form.

A sleep paralysis experience would settle for you the question of your existential validity once and for all. If indeed you can be aware of yourself as separate from the body, as being in a dimension which does not permit you to operate the body, then your individuality apart from the body is assured. Death then is meaningless in terms of it being the end of the person. Death is the end of the body habitat of the person.

Besides these two components of the sleep paralysis namely the body which cannot be operated and the person who cannot operate the body, there is one other component which we should observe. This is the life force in the physical body. We can recognize the authority of this life force very easily since its failure to fuse the person into the sleeping body, caused the state of paralysis.

If this life force operated in the expected way always, we would perhaps never understand ourselves as individual persons apart from the body habitats with which we identify. In that sense the malfunction of this life force serves our interest in removing the natural unity we have with the body. It may become the cause of psyche-realization.

Nature established this system of separation and fusion of the psychological functions and the physical body in such a way, that the person has little or no knowledge of the program. Understanding this system would require mental sensitivity which may bring clarity of the process. If during a paralysis one does not panic, if one reserves some objectivity, one may perceive the distinctions.

Sleep paralysis occurs on two occasions, namely, when one is about to separate from the body and when one is about to fuse into the body. These conditions are known to us as falling asleep and waking up.

In falling asleep, it is hardly likely that one will observe the distinctions in the incidence. One has a better opportunity while waking up. While waking one discovers oneself either waking after a dream or just waking with no memory of a mental or emotional experience. When it is after a dream, there is usually more opportunity to be objective.

During a dream one is usually so involved in the experience, that one fails to distinguish oneself from the occurrence. One participates without objectivity. However as soon as one tries to wake up as the physical body and one finds that it does not respond, one becomes alert immediately. The alertness does not stop the paralysis, but in fact, highlights it even more. One may be distressed to realize that even though one is consciously aware, even more so than in the dream state, still one cannot operate as the body. It is as though something prohibited one from being the body which one was before.

When the paralysis occurs after a dream, one may not realize that one is objectively struggling to animate the physical system. Instead one will try to animate it without objectivity, without understanding that one is different to the body and needs to operate it but is prohibited from doing so by some unknown force. Actually it is not a prohibition but it will be experienced as if it were so. It is simply a mismatch in the frequencies of the dream body and the physical one.

No one is there stopping you from operating the physical body but your will power is not reconnected with the nervous system of the physical body. Thus your commands cannot be executed.

Instead of panicking during a sleep paralysis experience, one should train the self to be objective and to draw conclusions. It should be that upon returning to the physical body after being in the dream world, the dreamer thinks, that he or she was unable to operate the body because the nervous system was not psychically connected to the will power.

The dreamer did not separate the two bodies. They separated naturally when the physical body required sleep. Thus whatever agency separated the bodies, that same operation would again re-unify them. The dreamer only has to do something to facilitate that involuntary action.

If the dreamer has no recall of dreams when the sleep paralysis is discovered just before waking, then the dreamer should assume that it had dreams which were not recalled, after which it was not fused properly with the physical system.

When sleep paralysis occurs while going to sleep, the person is neither in a state of being the physical body or the dreamer. This is very troublesome if you do not have the confidence of yourself as a psychological unit which is housed in a physical body.

In this type of paralysis, you are drifting into sleep, you doze off and you partially awakened in a semi-conscious state. You feel restrained and discover that you cannot move the physical body. At the same time, due to the drowsy condition, you feel very tired as if you do not have the strength to move the physical system.

This powerlessness is misinterpreted by the dreamer as a lack of strength to move the physical body. Actually all strength of the physical body is there. The willpower of the person is there. Therefore it is the disconnection between the willpower and the physical body which causes the impotency.

In the process of going to sleep, a person usually switches from full consciousness to partial consciousness, to full consciousness, to semi consciousness, to loss of awareness. These occur intermittently, until there is complete loss of objectivity. If however nature causes the person to be separated from the body while the person is still aware of the body, then that may be interpreted as sleep paralysis. It does happen on occasion that the person is simultaneously separated from the body and can also operate the body. That experience is part of a lucid dream situation. In that condition no powerless-ness is felt.

If while going to sleep one finds oneself in a sleep paralysis situation and then one falls asleep, one may remember the experience after sleeping. In some situations, persons paralyzed when falling sleep, make an effort to wake up. If they wake up they avoid going back to sleep immediately.

Others who try to move the body find that they are powerless to do so. They either fall asleep or fall into a dream experience and then wake up with or without remembering the paralysis experience.

Chapter 5

Realization of the Subtle Body

The benefit one may derive from sleep paralysis is the realization that one has a subtle body, which has psychological functions as its content. This subtle body, even though it seems to be ephemeral, is real nevertheless. The reality of it is counterbalanced by the physical system which is definitely perishable. The advantage of the physical body is its grossness. This quality gives us confidence in physical reality. We should, however, develop perception of subtle objects.

Since by nature's magic the subtle system and the physical one are fused during waking states and diffused during sleep, it is a challenge to study the process. Nature first puts the person to sleep and then does its magic of disengaging the subtle and gross bodies. By nature's magic a person is awake as a physical body, loses awareness in the process of falling asleep, becomes conscious again in a dream state, and then becomes awake again as the physical system.

The only way one can understand this is to be conscious while the body dozes and during dream states. One may think that most people are conscious during dreams states. Undoubtedly they are but that consciousness is usually different to the waking state. We need to be as objectively conscious during dreams as we are in the waking state. We need to discover ourselves in dream states so that we become conscious while dreaming either in a real astral world or in an imagined faculty.

There is this idea that all dream states are conditions of imagination. Some feel they are only thought constructions. This idea should be abandoned. Instead we should use the concept that we have both real astral realms and a mind which imagines. Physically we know that there are at least two realities, the physical one and the imaginative one which is local to the individual mind. The physical environment is shared by millions of living beings on the planet, while the imaginative environment is mostly shared by the individual alone.

The astral world like the physical reality, is shared by many entities. It exists independent of any limited being's dream. Is there a way through which we can increase objectivity during dream experiences? That would help considerably, first in sorting what is astral reality and what is imagination. How can we increase the degree of awareness in a drowsy condition?

Meditation when used as a process to develop psychic sensitivity can help us to sort the components of consciousness which are involved in what we know ourselves to be, which is a material body.

When taking naps, especially when one is not drowsy, one may study the change from wakefulness to sleep. If you take a nap when you are not tired, when your physical body is refreshed, you may remain silently in the mind, observing the gradual decrease of objectivity.

How does one transit from wakefulness to sleep?

When this happens gradually how does one transit from wakefulness to semi-consciousness?

When does nature achieve the full unconscious state in which there is no recall even of a single psychic incidence?

When returning to the wakeful state, how does one shift from total ignorance of one's surroundings, to being partially awake and then fully conscious?

Chapter 6

Sleep Paralysis Reversed

I finished this booklet on the subject of sleep paralysis. I am actually hung up on the book waiting for some contributory illustrations by Sir Paul Castagna.

In any case, there is one thing which I have to put into this book before it is published which is what is called reverse sleep paralysis. I had an experience early this morning which caused me to take a more in-depth look at that condition.

Actually sleep paralysis became known only as a situation of the physical body even though the subtle body is involved. It is rare however for even a frequent astral projector to experience paralysis of the subtle body when it is away from the physical form in the astral world.

In the usual paralysis, the experience is when the astral body returned into the physical one and the person is unable to move or cause the physical body to rise. That inability is interpreted by the mind as a paralysis.

It really isn't but that is how the mind interprets the experience because of the presumption of thinking that the physical body should always respond as the person, as the subtle energies of the person, or as the psychological self of the person. In this usage psychological self means the subtle body in which the self is only one component.

In reverse sleep paralysis, the person finds that the subtle body is disabled while it is outside of the physical form, during an astral projection when the astral body is far away from the physical form. This also causes double vision, meaning vision of the material world and vision of the subtle world simultaneously or alternately in split second shots.

This is further proof that the self is neither its physical body nor its subtle body but that it is wired into the system of these bodies in a seemingly inexplicable way.

Here is what happened:

My physical body was in the city of Las Vegas sleeping. My subtle body was in South America in a place which is an astral jungle area. In that place I was with a relative of my physical body. I was showing him a giant iguana which lives in the area. Right now in that area, iguanas only get as large as 3 feet from tip of nose to end of tail. These astral iguanas were about 15 feet from tip of nose to end of tail. They do not attack astral humans. They are mostly vegetarians. They are however wary of humans.

As soon as the creature saw my relative and me, it moved away. I brought it to his attention. Soon after this I was in an area of South America where the mother of my body is currently living. She is deceased but she has a place in the astral world which she created.

She was with some other astral people who are deceased. They were at a church service. These are people who left their last bodies as Christians.

After speaking to my mother and some other astral people, I was again with this other relative where the iguanas were. He did not grow up in South America but he always wanted to be in that situation. He was curious about the environment and the wildlife of the area.

We were in an old building which was left behind by some wealthy colonial people many many years ago in the astral domain.

After going through the building, we found the last room in it. There my astral body became very heavy. I could hardly move any part of it. To lift a finger was like lifting an elephant. It was painful but not as in pain from a wound. It was pain of having to exert so much willpower to do something which took just a reflex previously.

My relative's astral body was not affected in that way. In fact he lost perception of my astral body because my astral body shifted out of the astral vibrational level he was on. For all practical purposes he felt that I had disappeared even though I was just four feet from him.

At this point I became aware of Marcia Beloved's body which was lying near to mine in Las Vegas. I could see her body but it was hazy. I then called to her to ask her how she got to that astral place.

This is when there was dual vision where I was simultaneously seeing into the astral place and into the physical dimension which was far away. Both visions were superimposed like if you are seeing two slides, which are shown simultaneously through a projector, one as a layer over the other. In this dual dimensional vision, my point of reference was the astral reality, so the physical perception was interpreted also as an astral reality. Actually there was no physical perception at all, because on the physical side the physical body sat up and was not looking in the direction of

Marcia's body, nor were the eyelids of it open. Thus it could not have seen physically.

The physical vision was actually astral vision of the physical body. Or more precisely astral vision of the dense astral energy of the physical body. Since this vision was happening simultaneously with the vision of the astral place in South America, it seemed to the astral perception that her body was in the astral place but it was not. This shows that the astral body is capable of dual perception and that it cannot always sort such multiple perceptions.

Hearing my physical voice inquiring, Marcia called out on the physical side but of course with no perception of anything on the astral side.

This is a case of reverse sleep paralysis where the astral body itself experiences a shut down or a rapid de-energization. This is also controlled by the kundalini life force which makes independent decisions. The kundalini is stationed in the living physical body but it has power over the subtle body even if that body is far away.

Why did the kundalini do this? That is a very good question? Do some research on this and see if you can provide a sensible answer.

Special Note:

The most important part of this experience was not even mentioned above but I will let you ponder over it:

Where was the discrimination during the experience?

The discrimination is a vital part of the psyche. It is obvious that the discrimination is not the core-self. But where it is located? Why was it not connected to the core-self during the experience especially to sort the dual vision?

If the core-self is a component in the psyche and if the discrimination is a psychic apparatus, how are they connected or disconnected. How can the core-self commit sensible actions if it does not have the discrimination?

Artist's Closing Remarks

Michael asked me to do some illustrations for this text as well as inject the closing remarks.

When these phenomena of sleep paralysis first began happening, as a child, I had no name for it, or understanding of what it meant, or what really was involved. About a year after I met Michael and received instruction about astral projection and meditation, back in the early seventies, a man in California appeared to me. His name was Saul.

And he "gave me a message" about my life. To make a long story short, one of the three things he passed on to me was that there was an experience I had as a child (ages 5-7) that was now of some importance to me. Quite by accident, and weeks later, I came to recall an incident that took place when I was about seven, where, upon waking from a dream in which I was being stabbed in the back with a long spear. Rather than waking in a startled way, I was simultaneously aware of the "dream", and the fact of lying in bed. I toggled between these two states, feeling what it felt like to die from the spear wound as well as what it felt like to be lying in bed. The experience remained with me all those years, but the understanding did not come until I made the connection that even though I knew what it felt like to die in this painful manner, I continue to exist. This is insight into the nature of the subtle body, the physical body and the relationship between the two.

In this book, Michael has laid out a really straightforward and insightful look at a phenomena which probably everyone experiences, but has no objective way of understanding. He made the sacrifice of tracking his efforts and experiences as well as giving practical solutions to this problem. We are very fortunate, as readers, to have some guidelines to follow rather than each having to try to reinvent the wheel.

As these may be the last words I write, let me just add that I wish to express my undying thanks and appreciation for the tremendous body of work that Michael Beloved has given. Not just with these books, but the amazing website, illustrations, personal responses, constant exemplary practice and most of all his patience with people like myself who continue to struggle with all aspects of this ongoing process.

Sincerely...Thank You,

Paul

A word about my illustrations: Most of them were done with a real pen on real paper and then digitally colored in Photoshop and digitally signed with "©". My other images were done with a stylus on the iPad or in Adobe Illustrator.

All unmarked images were done by the author in Adobe Illustrator.

Glossary

Ashram is a boarding residence for yoga students.

Astral projection is the condition of being projected out of or away from the physical body.

Bhastrika is a rapid breath infusion process which arouses the kundalini life force.

Chakras are energy vortexes in the subtle body.

Death is the total shutdown of the physical body habitat of the person.

Higue is an elderly woman who sucks blood from sleeping infants because her infirm body no longer produces blood.

Jumbie is a creole term for a mischievous disembodied spirit.

Kundalini life force is stationed at the base of the spine in a human being. This force operates the body. It controls the sleep-wake cycle. It is responsible for the fission and fusion of the subtle and gross bodies

Life force, known also as kundalini, is psychic instinct mechanism which is located at the base of the spine. This force operates the body. It controls the sleep-wake cycle. It is responsible for the fission and fusion of the subtle and gross forms.

Lucid dreaming occurs when someone experiences the subtle existence while being fully conscious of the physical body.

Rapid breathing is a rapid breath infusion process which arouses the kundalini life force.

Reverse sleep paralysis is the condition of not being able to operate the subtle body during an astral projection while it is displaced from the physical system.

Silver cord is an energy transmission line from the life force in the physical body to the separated subtle form. If an alarm is sounded when the two bodies are separated, the kundalini uses that transmission conduit to yank the subtle body back into fusion with the physical system

Sleep paralysis is the condition of not being able to operate the physical body even though one is conscious within it.

Index

A

afterlife, 12

alcohol, 44

alcoholic, 53

altered states, 9

ancestors, 60

apple, 17

armature, 23

artist, author, 78

asafetida, 30

ashram, 36

astral landscape, 17

astral projection body, 12

astral reach, 56

astral stuffs, 12

astral vibratory rate, 54

astral vision, physical body, 78

author,

> artist, 78

> childhood, 26

> father, 44

> incidence decrease, 6

B

background, 12

bag, 12

Beloved, Marcia, 77

Bhajan, Yogi, 35

bhastrika pranayama, 36

blackout, 52

blood distribution, 38

breath mechanism, 33

breath suspension, 29

C

cell repair, 52

chakras, vortex, 35

chemicals of nature, 9

chemicals, 54

childhood, sleep paralysis, 8

cocaine, 54

Colorado, 35

condiment, 30

conquer nature, 38

consciousness,

> geography, 9

> malfunction, 8

constipation, 55, 56

copper wire, 23

copper wire, 23

cyberspace, 6

D

demon possession, 58

Denver, 35

depressed person, 53

desire, 10,15

digestion, 38

discernment, 17

disembodied spirit, 32

distances, 26

distended stomach, 50

dizziness, 34

dream body, 12

dream casing, 7

dream experience, 13

dream outside mind, 15

dream recall, decrease, 51

dream states, 70

dreams, imaginary, 16

drinking alcohol, 44

drug addict, 53

drug applied, 26

dual vision, 77

E

eating late, 50

electrician, 24

electricity, 23

emotions, body, 13

energy cortex, 35

energy transmission, 35

epilepsy, 6, 54

epileptic bouts, 58

equator, 27

etheric body, 12

existence, factor, 33

F

factors, four, 33

failed reentry, 31

falling asleep, 63

falling, 26

father, 44

filtration, 47

fission system, 61

food processing, 52

fresh air access, 46

fruit, 17

function of nature, 8

G

gas, 48

geography of nature, 9

God, 28

Gopi Krishna, 35

graveyards, 27

H

hallucinogenic drugs, 54

hereafter, 12

higues, 29

honesty, 18

horror movies, 42

I

identity energy, 14

iguana, 75

Illustrator, 82

imaginary dreams, 16

imagination, 10, 15

imagine an idea, 17

introspective study, 8

involuntary breathing, 39

iPad, 82

J, K, L

jolted, 20

jumbie, 32

Kansas City, 35

knees, 27

Krishna, Gopi, 35

kundalini,

astral body controlled, 78

location, 34

landscape, 17

larger, 28

Las Vegas, 75

learning to walk, 26

life force,

control, 38

location, 34

lifeline, 37

loud noise, 19

low energy persons, 53

lucid dreaming, 23, 67

lungs function, 49

M

manic states, 54

Marcia Beloved, 77

marijuana, 54

memory, 10, 15

mental delirium, 54

mental force body, 13

mento-emotional body, 12

Michael, 78

mind body, 12

mind-altering, 54

misidentification, 14

Missouri, 35

moon, 9

N, O

nature,

>   beyond control, 8

>   to conquer, 38

>   magic, 69

nerve failure, 19

noise, 19

opium, 54

other world, 21

outer space, 9

P, Q

painkillers, 56

paralysis events, 58

perception, multiple, 78

performance, astral, 17

person as psychology, 22

personality, psychological, 60

Philippines, 30

Photoshop, 82

poisonous gas, 48

pranayama, 36

psychic research, 9

psychic substance, 43

psychoactive substances, 54

psychological content body, 12

psychological part, 21

R

Rampa, 31

rapid breathing, 36

recurrence, 45

reentry, 31

reincarnation, 33

research, psychic, 9

reserve sleep paralysis, 74

romantic affairs, 16

S

Saul, 78

self, component, 74

self-honesty, 18

sensation body, 13

sensations, 34

shadow body, 12

shivering, 34

silver cord, 35

skin, 12

sleep paralysis,

      childhood, 8

      defined, 18, 22

      elimination, 41

      lucid dreaming, 23

      occasion, 13

      recurrence, 45

      separated, 14

sleep walks, 49

slip back, 29

South America, 75

spear wound, 81

spirit possession, 29

spirit, disembodied, 32

stomach, 50

stroke, 19

stuff of feeling, 12

stuff of reason, 12

stuff of sensation, 12

stuff of thinking, 12

stylus, 82

subtle body,

       components, 12

       distinct, 21

       factor, 33

       heavy, 77

       kundalini controls, 78

       packed, 13

       paralyzed, 77

       premise, 9

       synchronize, 7

subtle dimension, 11

surgery, 9

suspicious of the dark, 27

synchronization, jolted, 20

synthetic chemicals, 54

T, U, V, W, X, Y, Z

T. Lobsang Rampa, 31

third eye, 31

train yourself, 61

transmission line, 35

ventilation, 46

verge of sleeping/waking, 7

vision, dual, 77

vocal cord, 29

vodka, 45

waking up, 63

waking/sleeping, 7

walk, 26

will power, ineffective, 19

Yogi Bhajan, 35

Author

Michael Beloved (Yogi *Madhvacarya)* took his current body in 1951 in Guyana. During infancy and childhood he had many conscious astral projections as well as sleep paralysis bouts which lasted for the most about 2 minutes. He assumed that this was a natural state and that each person overcomes this in the process of time just as infants have an imbalance when learning to walk but master it nevertheless even if they lack confidence. During the early teen years, Michael tried to study sleep paralysis on his own without mentioning anything to senior relatives. In 1965, while living in Trinidad, he instinctively began doing yoga postures and tried to make sense of the supernatural side of life.

Later in 1970, in the Philippines, he approached a Martial Arts Master named Mr. Arthur Beverford. He explained to the teacher that he was seeking a yoga instructor. Mr. Beverford identified himself as an advanced disciple of Rishi Singh Gherwal, an ashtanga yoga master.

Beverford taught the traditional Ashtanga Yoga with stress on postures, attentive breathing and brow chakra centering meditation. In 1972, Michael entered the Denver Colorado Ashram of *kundalini* yoga Master Harbhajan Singh. There he took instruction in bhastrika pranayama and its application to yoga postures. He was supervised mostly by Yogi Bhajan's disciple named Prem Kaur.

After learning kundalini yoga, Michael realized that sleep paralysis was caused by the kundalini life force's inability to synchronize the subtle and gross bodies. He investigated the cause of this and discovered that if the kundalini was kept in a super charged state, sleep paralysis would not occur.

Publications

English Series

Bhagavad Gita English

Anu Gita English

Markandeya Samasya English

Yoga Sutras English

Uddhava Gita English

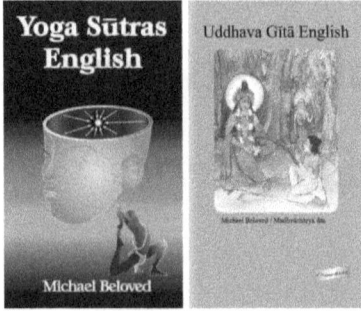

These are in 21ˢᵗ Century English, very precise and exacting. Many Sanskrit words which were considered untranslatable into a Western language are rendered in precise, expressive and modern English, due to the English language becoming the world's universal means of concept conveyance.

Three of these books are instructions from Krishna. **In Bhagavad Gita English** and **Anu Gita English**, the instructions were for Arjuna. In the **Uddhava Gita English,** it was for Uddhava. Bhagavad Gita and Anu Gita are extracted from the Mahabharata. Uddhava Gita was extracted from the 11ᵗʰ Canto of the Srimad Bhagavatam (Bhagavata Purana). One of these books, the **Markandeya Samasya English** is about Krishna, as described by Yogi Markandeya, who survived the cosmic collapse and reached a divine child in whose transcendental body, the collapsed world was existing. Another of these books, the **Yoga Sutras English,** is the detailed syllabus about yoga practice.

My suggestion is that you read **Bhagavad Gita English**, the **Anu Gita English, the Markandeya Samasya English,** the **Yoga Sutras English** and lastly the **Uddhava Gita English**, which is much more complicated and detailed.

For each of these books we have at least one commentary, which is published separately. Thus your particular interest can be researched further in the commentaries.

The smallest of these commentaries and perhaps the simplest is the one for the Anu Gita. We published its commentary as the Anu Gita Explained. The Bhagavad Gita explanations were published in three distinct targeted commentaries. The first is Bhagavad Gita Explained, which sheds lights on how people in the time of Krishna and Arjuna regarded the information and applied it. Bhagavad Gita is an exposition of the application of yoga practice to cultural activities, which is known in the Sanskrit language as karma yoga.

Interestingly, Bhagavad Gita was spoken on a battlefield just before one of the greatest battles in the ancient world. A warrior, Arjuna, lost his wits and had no idea that he could apply his training in yoga to political dealings. Krishna, his charioteer, lectured on the spur of the moment to give Arjuna the skill of using yoga proficiency in cultural dealings including how to deal with corrupt officials on a battlefield.

The second commentary is the Kriya Yoga Bhagavad Gita. This clears the air about Krishna's information on the science of kriya yoga, showing that its techniques are clearly described free of charge to anyone who takes the time to read Bhagavad Gita. Kriya yoga concerns the battlefield which is the psyche of the living being. The internal war and the mental and emotional forces which are hostile to self-realization are dealt with in the kriya yoga practice.

The third commentary is the Brahma Yoga Bhagavad Gita. This shows what Krishna had to say outright and what he hinted about which concerns the brahma yoga practice, a mystic process for those who mastered kriya yoga.

There is one commentary for the **Markandeya Samasya English**. The title of that publication is Krishna Cosmic Body.

There are two commentaries to the Yoga Sutras. One is the Yoga Sutras of Patanjali and the other is the Meditation Expertise. These give detailed explanations of the process of Yoga.

For the Uddhava Gita, we published the Uddhava Gita Explained. This is a large book and requires concentration and study for integration of the information. Of the books which deal with transcendental topics, my opinion is that the discourse between Krishna and Uddhava has the complete information about the realities in existence. This book is the one which removes massive existential ignorance.

Meditation Series

Meditation Pictorial

Meditation Expertise

Core-Self Discovery

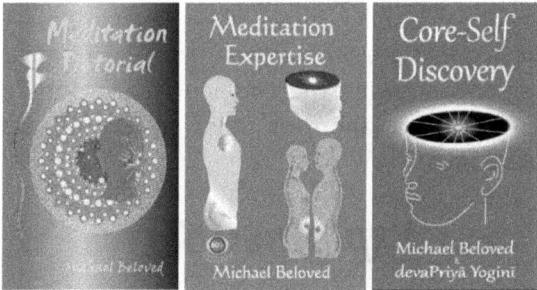

The specialty of these books is the mind diagrams which profusely illustrate what is written. This shows exactly what one has to do mentally to develop and then sustain a meditation practice.

In the **Meditation Pictorial**, one is shown how to develop psychic insight, a feature without which meditation is imagination and visualization, without any mystic experience per se.

In the **Meditation Experti**se, one is shown how to corral one's practice to bring it in line with the classic syllabus of yoga which Patanjali lays out as the ashtanga yoga eight-staged practice.

In **Core-Self Discovery**, one is taken though the course of pratyahar sensual energy withdrawal which is the 5th stage of yoga in the Patanjali ashtanga eight-process complete system of yoga practice. These events lead to the discovery of a core-self which is surrounded by psychic organs in the head of the subtle body. This product has a DVD component for teachers and self-teaching students.

These books are profusely illustrated with mind diagrams showing the components of psychic consciousness and the inner design of the subtle body.

Explained Series

Bhagavad Gita Explained

Uddhava Gita Explained

Anu Gita Explained

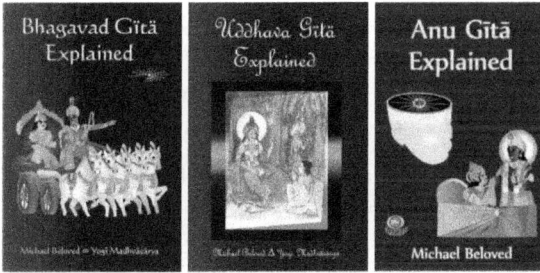

The specialty of these books is that they are free of missionary intentions, cult tactics and philosophical distortion. Instead of using these books to add credence to a philosophy, meditation process, belief or plea for followers, I spread the information out so that a reader can look through this literature and freely take or leave anything as desired.

When Krishna stressed himself as God, I stated that. When Krishna laid no claims for supremacy, I showed that. The reader is left to form an independent opinion about the validity of the information and the credibility of Krishna.

There is a difference in the discourse with Arjuna in the Bhagavad Gita and the one with Uddhava in the Uddhava Gita. In fact these two books may appear to contradict each other. In the Bhagavad Gita, Krishna pressured Arjuna to complete social duties. In the Uddhava Gita, Krishna insisted that Uddhava should abandon the same.

The Anu Gita is not as popular as the Bhagavad Gita but it is the conclusion of that text. Anu means what is to follow, what proceeds. In this discourse, an anxious Arjuna request that Krishna should repeat the Bhagavad Gita and again show His supernatural and divine forms.

However Krishna refuses to do so and chastises Arjuna for being a disappointment in forgetting what was revealed. Krishna then cites a celestial yogi, a near-perfected being, who explained the process of transmigration in vivid detail.

Commentaries

Yoga Sutras of Patanjali

Meditation Expertise

Krishna Cosmic Body

Anu Gita Explained

Bhagavad Gita Explained

Kriya Yoga Bhagavad Gita

Brahma Yoga Bhagavad Gita

Uddhava Gita Explained

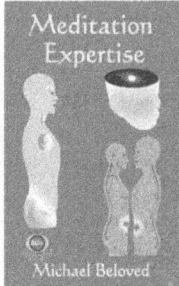

Yoga Sutras of Patanjali is the globally acclaimed text book of yoga. This has detailed expositions of yoga techniques. Many kriya techniques are vividly described in the commentary.

Meditation Expertise is an analysis and application of the Yoga Sutras. This book is loaded with illustrations and has detailed explanations of secretive advanced meditation techniques which are called kriyas in the Sanskrit language.

Krishna Cosmic Body is a narrative commentary on the Markandeya Samasya portion of the Aranyaka Parva of the Mahabharata. This is the detailed description of the dissolution of the world, as experienced by the great yogin Markandeya who transcended the cosmic deity, Brahma, and reached Brahma's source who is the divine infant, Krishna.

Anu Gita Explained is a detailed explanation of how we endure many material bodies in the course of transmigrating through various life-forms. This is a discourse between Krishna and Arjuna. Arjuna requested of Krishna a display of the Universal Form and a repeat narration of the Bhagavad Gita but Krishna declined and explained what a siddha perfected being told the Yadu family about the sequence of existences one endures and the systematic flow of those lives at the convenience of material nature.

Bhagavad Gita Explained shows what was said in the Gita without religious overtones and sectarian biases.

Kriya Yoga Bhagavad Gita shows the instructions for those who are doing kriya yoga.

Brahma Yoga Bhagavad Gita shows the instructions for those who are doing brahma yoga.

Uddhava Gita Explained shows the instructions to Uddhava which are more advanced than the ones given to Arjuna.

Bhagavad Gita is an instruction for applying the expertise of yoga in the cultural field. This is why the process taught to Arjuna is called karma yoga which means karma + yoga or cultural activities done with a yogic demeanor.

Uddhava Gita is an instruction for apply the expertise of yoga to attaining spiritual status. This is why it is explains jnana yoga and bhakti yoga in detail. Jnana yoga is using mystic skill for knowing the spiritual part of existence. Bhakti yoga is for developing affectionate relationships with divine beings.

Karma yoga is for negotiating the social concerns in the material world and therefore it is inferior to bhakti yoga which concerns negotiating the social concerns in the spiritual world.

This world has a social environment and the spiritual world has one too.

Right now Uddhava Gita is the most advanced informative spiritual book on the planet. There is nothing anywhere which is superior to it or which goes into so much detail as it. It verified that historically Krishna is the most advanced human being to ever have left literary instructions on this planet. Even Patanjali Yoga Sutras which I translated and gave an application for in my book, **Meditation Expertise**, does not go as far as the Uddhava Gita.

Some of the information of these two books is identical but while the Yoga Sutras are concerned with the personal spiritual emancipation (kaivalyam) of the individual spirits, the Uddhava Gita explains that and also explains the situations in the spiritual universes.

Bhagavad Gita is from the Mahabharata which is the history of the Pandavas. Arjuna, the student of the Gita, is one of the Pandavas brothers. He was in a social hassle and did not know how to apply yoga expertise to solve it. Krishna gave him a crash-course on the battlefield about that.

Uddhava Gita is from the Srimad Bhagavatam (Bhagavata Purana), which is a history of the incarnations of Krishna. Uddhava was a relative of Krishna. He was concerned about the situation of the deaths of many of his relatives but Krishna diverted Uddhava's attention to the practice of yoga for the purpose of successfully migrating to the spiritual environment.

Specialty

These books are based on the author's experiences in meditation, yoga practice and participation in spiritual groups:

Spiritual Master

sex you!

Sleep **Paralysis**

Astral Projection

Masturbation Psychic Details

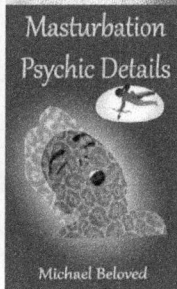

In **Spiritual   Master**, Michael   draws   from experience with gurus or with their senior students. His contact with astral gurus is rated. He walks you through the avenue of gurus showing what you should do and what you should not do, so as to gain proficiency in whatever area of spirituality the guru has proficiency.

sex you! is a masterpiece about the adventures of an individual spirit's passage through the parents' psyches. The conversion of a departed soul into a sexual urge is described. The transit from the afterlife to residency in the emotions of the parents is detailed. This is about sex and you; learn about how much of you comprises the romantic energy of your would-be parents!

Sleep Paralysis clears misconceptions so that one can see what sleep paralysis is and what frightening astral experience occurs while the paralysis   is   being   experienced.   This disempowerment has great value in giving you confidence that you can and do exist even if you are unable to operate the physical body. The implication is that one can exist apart from and will survive the loss of the material body.

Astral Projection details experiences Michael had even in childhood, where he assumed incorrectly   that   everyone   was   astrally conversant. He discusses the life force psychic mechanism which operates the sleep-wake cycle of the physical form, and which budgets energy into the separated astral form which determines if the individual will have dream recall or no objective awareness during the projections. Astral travel happens on every occasion when the physical body sleeps. What is missing in awareness is the observer status while the astral body is separated.

Masturbation Psychic Details is a surprise presentation which relates what happens on the psychic plane during a masturbation event. This does not tackle moral issues or even addictions but shows the involvement of memory and the sure but hidden subconscious mind which operates many features of the psyche irrespective of the desire or approval of the self-conscious personality.

Online Resources

Visit The Website And Forum

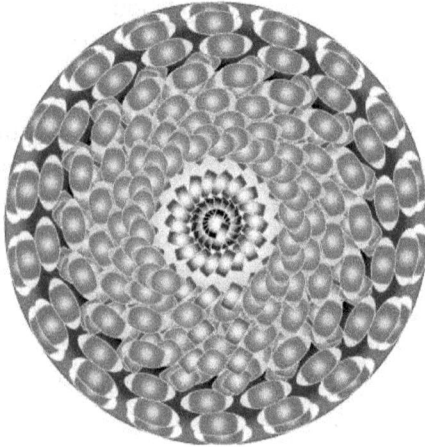

Email:	michaelbelovedbooks@gmail.com
	axisnexus@gmail.com

Website	michaelbeloved.com
Forum:	inselfyoga.com